W9-BJK-201

DATE DUE

ART OF THE MIDDLE AGES

Jennifer Olmsted

Heinemann Library
Chicago, Illinois

©2001 Reed Educational & Professional Publishing
Published by Heinemann Library,
an imprint of Reed Educational & Professional Publishing,
Chicago, IL

Customer Service 888-454-2279

Visit our website at www.heinemannlibrary.com

Printed in China

05 04 03 02 01
10 9 8 7 6 5 4 3 2 1

Library of Congress Cataloging-in-Publication Data
Olmsted, Jennifer.
  Art of the middle ages / Jennifer Olmsted.
    p. cm. -- (Art in history)
Includes bibliographical references and index.
  ISBN 1-58810-091-X
  1. Art, Medieval--Juvenile literature. [1. Art, Medieval.] I. Title.
II. Art in history (Chicago, Ill.)
  N5975 .O45 2001
  709'.02--dc21
                     00-012476

Acknowledgments
The author and the publisher are grateful to the following for permission to reproduce copyright photographs: © Art Resource/The Pierpont Morgan Library, p. 20; © Art Resource/Scala, p. 13; © *Duke William and his Fleet Cross the Channel to Pevensey,* 11th century (embroidery), Musee de la Tapisserie, Bayeux, France/Visual Arts Library, London/Bridgeman Art Library, p. 5; *The Story of Thamyris,* from *'De Claris Mulieribus'* Works of Giovanni Boccaccio (1313-75), Bibliotheque Notionale, Paris, France/Bridgeman Art Library, p. 7; © The Bridgeman Art Library Int'l. Ltd. (U.S.)/ Cathedral of Notre Dame, Reims, France, p. 25; *Joachim among the Sheperds,* c. 1305 (fresco) (for detail see 65213) by Giotto di Bondone (c. 1266-1337), Scrovegni (Arena) Chapel, Padua, Italy/The Bridgeman Art Library, p. 28; © British Library/Carpet page. Lindisfarne, p. 9; © By permission of British Museum, p. 8; © Corbis/Archivo Iconografico, S.A., p. 10; © Corbis/Dave Bartruff, p. 15; © Corbis/Bettmann, p. 11; © Corbis/Dean Conger, p. 18; © Corbis/Marc Garanger, p. 14; © Corbis/Angelo Hornak, p. 16; © Corbis/Richard List, p. 17; © Corbis/National Gallery Collection; By kind permission of the Trustees of the National Gallery, London, p. 29; © Corbis/Vanni Archive/Ruggero Vanni, pp. 12, 24; © Corbis/Gian Berto Vanni, p. 26; © The Granger Collection, p. 22; © Metropolitan Museum of Art/The Metropolitan Museum of Art, The Cloisters Collection, 1954. (54.1.2) Photograph © 1991, p. 23; © Courtesy of Niedersachsisches Landemuseum, p. 6; © Uppsala Universitetsbibliotek/Reprosektionen, p. 21; © The Walters Art Gallery, Baltimore, p. 19.

Every effort has been made to contact copyright holders of any material reproduced in this book. Any omissions will be rectified in subsequent printings if notice is given to the publisher.

Special thanks to Dr. Kelly Holbert for her comments in the preparation of this book.

Some words are shown in bold, **like this.**
You can find out what they mean by looking in the glossary.

CONTENTS

WHAT IS THE MIDDLE AGES?

The Middle Ages is the time period from about 400 C.E. to about 1400 C.E. in Europe. The word **medieval** is used to describe something that came from the Middle Ages.

The early Middle Ages

There was a lot of unrest in Europe from about 500 C.E. to 1000 C.E. Settled people in western Europe fought with **migratory** groups for land that had once been ruled by the Roman Empire. Gradually the migratory people began to settle into their new lands. Many became Christians. Christianity was a new religion that was slowly spreading through Europe.

Three periods of art

Medieval art is usually divided into three main periods:
- Early Medieval, 400–1050 C.E.;
- **Romanesque**, 1050–1200 C.E.; and
- **Gothic**, 1150–1400 C.E.

Some of these periods overlap each other. The Early Medieval period features a mixture of Christian and migratory styles and subjects. The Romanesque period has buildings that are simple and weighty, and art that is full of movement. In the Gothic period, buildings focus on height, light, and color, and art becomes more elegant and refined.

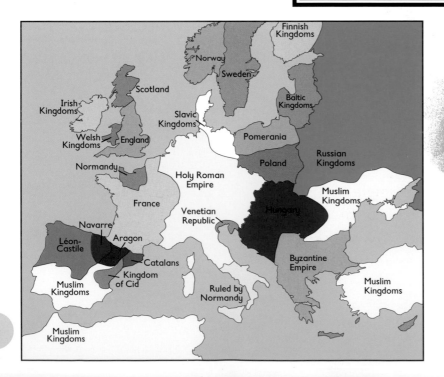

This map shows Europe around 1100 C.E. Medieval Europe was made up of many different small kingdoms and states.

:O:NAVIGIO:

MAR E

Duke William and his Fleet Cross the Channel to Pevensey, *detail from the* Bayeux Tapestry, *wool embroidery on linen, height 20 in. (50.8 cm) length 229 ft. 8 in. (70 m) ca. 1070–1080 C.E.*

The later Middle Ages

After about 1000 C.E., lords, kings, and leaders of the church fought for control of the towns and farmland. The **tapestry** on this page tells the story of one of these battles, the **Norman** conquest of England in 1066 C.E. Sometimes kings and church leaders joined forces. The **Crusades,** a series of wars that began in 1095 C.E. between the Christians of Europe and the Muslims in the Middle East, were an example of this. After 1150 C.E. the Christian church became very strong. With the help of the church, the French kingdom became the most powerful country in Western Europe.

In this scene of the tapestry you can see the Norman soldiers and their horses riding in ships on their way to do battle in England.

MATERIALS AND METHODS

Medieval artists

During the Middle Ages, most artists were either **monks** or **artisans.** Monks are men who live shut away from the world in **monasteries,** to pray and serve God. Artisans are ordinary people whose job is making art. Some medieval artisans lived and worked in one town all their lives. Others traveled from town to town. Until the twelfth century, most people who made art were monks. Later, artisans took over the making of art. During the **Gothic** period, all craftsmen, including artisans, belonged to **guilds.** Guilds controlled the pricing and sale of art, and controlled the training of artisans. The guilds also supported the families of guild members who died.

Masons were craftsmen who specialized in stonework. Working with architects, they designed churches and directed the workers who built them. Many masons belonged to guilds.

Artisans rarely signed their works. People in the Middle Ages made art to honor God or kings. The person who made the art wasn't important.

A Monk carving a choir stall, wooden panel from a choir stall, Germany, 1284 C.E.

The monk uses a hammer and chisel to carve a wooden seat. Other tools hang on the wall beside him.

Artists' materials

Medieval artists worked with many different materials. They sometimes painted on walls and wood panels, but few of these survive. More often, artists painted on treated animal skins, called **parchment** or **vellum,** which were bound into books. To make paint, artists had to grind **pigments** and then mix them with resin, a liquid made from tree sap; water; egg yolk; or, more rarely, oil. Brushes were made out of animal hair or fur that was tied to the quill of a feather or a wooden stick.

Sculptors and woodworkers used stone and wood to make statues. Artists made beautiful objects out of glass, ivory, enamel, gold, silver, and bronze. Other kinds of artists made **tapestries,** which were painstakingly woven and sometimes embroidered.

> **Women artists**
> Most artists were men, but there were some women artists. Nuns sometimes made books and paintings. Women also made tapestries and textiles.

The story of Thamyris, page from a copy of Boccaccio's De Claris Mulieribus (Book of Renowned Women), *1402 C.E.*

This **illumination** shows a woman painting while her apprentice grinds pigments.

LOCAL TRADITIONS

Art of early Europe

During the early Middle Ages, both settled and **migratory** people made beautiful objects. As in ancient times, jewelry was one of the most common types of art. **Artisans** made pins, buckles, knife handles, crowns, weapons, and mirrors out of gold, silver, and bronze. Sometimes they added precious gems and **enamel.** Their workmanship was of a very high quality.

Some northern people, like the Vikings, made complicated wood carvings for their ships, houses, beds, and other belongings. The Vikings also carved and painted stones with pictures of battles and folktales.

The **Saxons** also used a complicated pattern for decoration. It is called **interlace,** because it looks like ribbons twisted and woven together.

Golden buckle of Sutton Hoo, length 5¼ in. (13.4 cm) England, ca. 600–700 C.E.

This golden belt buckle was found in the buried treasury of a king named Raedwald. He ruled in the time before Christianity had reached all of England. The patterns in the gold are interlace patterns.

Local traditions and the new religion

At the same time that early **medieval** peoples made art, Christianity began to spread from Rome to the rest of Europe. Local art forms changed as people embraced the new religion. People in different regions took Christian **symbols,** like the cross, and added their own decorations to them. Much religious art was made with patterns and themes that came from local arts.

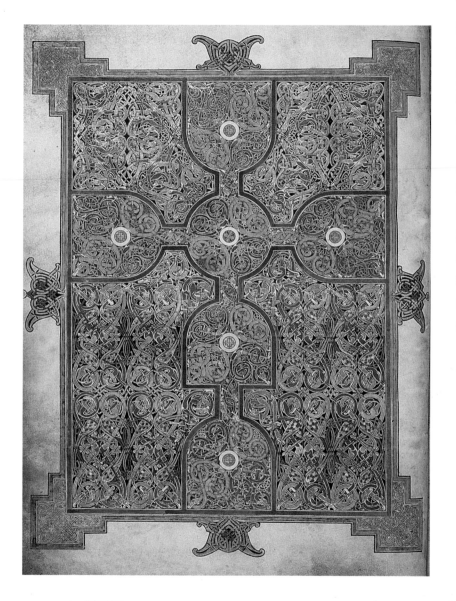

This beautiful page from a book is called a "carpet page" because it looks like an oriental carpet. The artists who made this page used a cross, an important Christian symbol. They combined this new symbol with their own local tradition of interlace.

Carpet page with a cross, illustration from the Lindisfarne Gospels, *England, 13¹/₂ in. x 9¹/₄ in. (34.3 cm x 23.5 cm) ca. 700 C.E.*

SYMBOLS AND STORIES

The break with tradition

In ancient Greece and Rome, people preferred art that looked very lifelike and natural. During the Middle Ages, lifelike qualities were much less important. **Medieval** art focused on the ideas behind the images. **Symbolism** and stories were very important because they helped explain these ideas. The painting on this page shows Christ on a throne. Several symbols tell us that he is Christ: the **halo** with the cross in it, the open book on his lap, his hand gesture, and the **mandorla** that surrounds him. Along with Christ's rich robes and fierce expression, these symbols encouraged awe and respect.

Christ in Majesty, *wall painting from the* **apse** *of San Clemente of Tahull, Spain, ca. 1123 C.E.*

This image of Christ is painted on the ceiling of a church, so that people could look up during the service and remember why it was important to worship God.

This page shows the story of Christ's birth. He and his mother, Mary, both have halos to show that they are holy.

Subjects and symbols

A great deal of medieval art was about themes from the Bible. Some art also showed the lives of saints and church leaders. Medieval artists used Christian symbols that are still used today. One important symbol in medieval art is the cross. It is the most important Christian symbol because it is a symbol for the death and **resurrection** of Jesus Christ. The halo, another important symbol, is a sign of holiness. It is used only for images of Jesus, his family, God, and the saints.

Art that tells stories

Medieval artists made paintings and sculptures that told stories from the Bible. Most people in the Middle Ages could not read. Art helped them learn about God because it used pictures instead of words to tell stories. Symbols helped people figure out who was who in the pictures.

ART FOR CHURCHES

Churches were very important places for art during the Middle Ages. Most art was made for churches. Church leaders, kings, and noblemen hired artists to do this. One reason for having art in churches was that art was a sign of **devotion.** Spending money on expensive materials and craftsmanship showed respect and honor for God.

Another reason for art in churches was that the church was a central space for all members of society. Rich and poor alike went to **Mass.** By telling stories in pictures, art taught them about Christianity. Art also persuaded people to become or remain Christians. It took a long time for Christianity to grow strong in Europe. Scenes like the one in the picture, sculpted above a **cathedral** door, showed frightening themes that encouraged people to be good Christians.

Last Judgment, by *Gislebertus*, **tympanum** and **lintel,** *Autun Cathedral, Germany, ca.1120–1135 C.E.*

This sculpture shows Christ separating the good Christians from the bad ones, to decide who would go to Heaven.

Celebrating Christianity

Many types of art were found in churches. Paintings appeared on the walls and ceilings of some churches. Churches often had sculptures inside and out. Sculptors carved scenes on columns, walls, and **portals.** They also made statues of holy figures. Sculptors who specialized in wood carved seats for the clergy. They also carved screens that separated parts of the church from each other. Metalworkers and ivory carvers made cups called chalices, plates called patens, and crosses. These objects were especially important because they were needed for the Mass.

The Altar of Saint Ambrose, *by Wolvinus, gold with enamel and gems, 2 ft. 9½ in. x 7 ft. ½ in. (80 cm x 213 cm) Sant'Ambrogio, Milan, Italy, ca. 824–866 C.E.*

The artist Wolvinus made this altar for an archbishop named Angilbert II who wanted to honor Saint Ambrose. The archbishop would have used the altar in the Mass.

ROMANESQUE CHURCHES

Many churches were built in Europe during the time known as the **Romanesque** period, from about 1050 C.E. to 1200 C.E. These churches shared some common features. Taken together, these features make up the Romanesque style. One important feature was the use of rounded arches above windows and doors. These arches also appeared in the ceilings of the churches, called vaults.

Another feature of the Romanesque style was the division of the church into separate parts. This allowed several activities to take place at the same time. Like earlier churches, Romanesque churches were built in the shape of a cross. The large central space in the church, called the **nave,** allowed large numbers of church members to hear the **Mass.** People prayed in small **chapels** in the wings of the church or **cathedral.** Sculptures often covered the spaces around the doorways.

Saint Sernin, *Toulouse, France, 1070–1096 C.E.*

The cathedral of Saint Sernin was an important church. Windows with rounded arches covered the outside of the building. You can also see the small chapels that were part of the church.

Buildings for pilgrims

Throughout the Middle Ages, people traveled to holy sites to show their faith. These people were called "pilgrims." During Romanesque times, the number of pilgrims grew very large. Pilgrims followed special routes across Europe and the Middle East to visit places where important religious events had taken place. Towns along these routes raised money to build huge churches. The churches were designed to hold large numbers of visiting pilgrims and local people. Many of these churches were built on the most important Christian sites. They also held the **relics** of saints.

Interior of the Cathedral Santiago de Compostela, *Spain, 1075–1120 C.E.*

This important cathedral was the end goal for many pilgrims. It held the tomb and relics of St. James.

Medieval pilgrims

In his book, *The Canterbury Tales,* the English poet Geoffrey Chaucer describes a character who had made most of the trips that pilgrims took in Romanesque and Gothic times:

And three times had she been at Jerusalem;
She had passed many a strange stream;
At Rome she had been, and at Bologna,
In France at St. James, and at Cologne.
She knew much of wandering by the way.

GOTHIC CHURCHES

The **Gothic** style in art and architecture began in France about 1150 C.E., and continued until the fifteenth century in some parts of Europe. Suger, the **abbot** of an important **monastery** in France, introduced many of the new ideas that led to the Gothic style in buildings. Suger had traveled a lot and seen many types of buildings. He worked closely with **masons** to develop new ideas. Saint Denis, the **abbey** church he helped build, was the first Gothic church in Europe.

Space and light

In the Gothic period, the heavy pillars of the **Romanesque** style were removed. Instead, masons used new supports called **buttresses** that held up the walls from the outside of the church. Masons used buttresses to build high, thin walls that made the churches seem open and airy inside. The sense of space created by the tall walls was emphasized by huge stained-glass windows that let in light. Inside, masons drew attention to the height of the church with small columns that ran from the floor to the ceiling.

Nave, Amiens Cathedral, *1220–1288 C.E., France, 136½ ft. (42 m) high.*

Masons used tall, thin columns and ceilings with pointed arches to make the church seem even taller than it was. Stained-glass windows let in light and color.

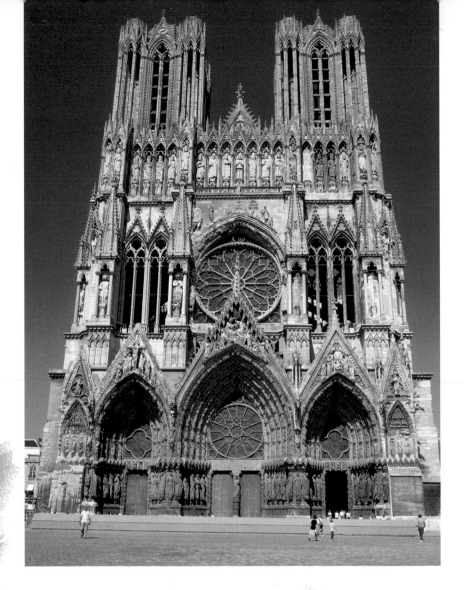

West side, Reims Cathedral, *France, 1220–1260 C.E.,* towers mid-fifteenth century.

Pointed arches and long, thin columns make the front of this church look very imposing. The huge round window at the front, called a rose window, fills the inside with colored light. There are many sculptures on the front of this church.

Another key feature of Gothic churches was the pointed arch above doors and windows on the outside of the church. The shape and slenderness of the arch drew the eye upwards. These arches also emphasized the height of the church. Gothic masons stressed height inside and outside the church because many people thought of the **cathedral** as the house of God, who lived up in the heavens. To make them even more beautiful, Gothic sculptors covered the fronts of churches with statues.

GOTHIC GLORY

Buttresses allowed **Gothic masons** to put large windows in church walls. These windows were made of stained glass. These beautiful windows filled the churches with color and light. The windows also had pictures that told stories.

How stained glass was made

First the metal outlines that held the glass were made. Then craftsmen mixed **pigments** with sand and other glass-making materials, and heated them until they melted together. After the sheet of colored glass cooled, they cut it into small pieces. Each sheet was only one color, so many different sheets were made. The small pieces of glass were placed in their proper places in the metal frame. Then everything was heated again to seal the glass to the metal.

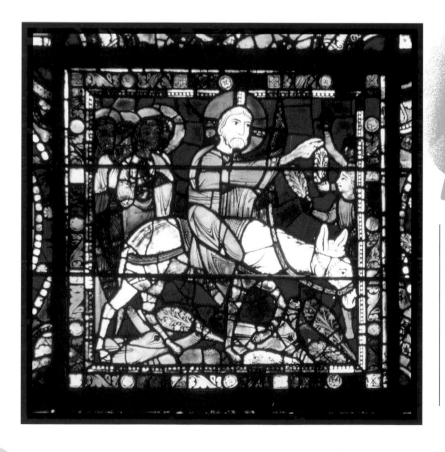

Christ Entering Jerusalem, *stained-glass window, west side of Chartres Cathedral, France, ca.1200–1236 C.E.*

This image is part of a window that illustrates the story of Christ's life. There are more than 100 stained-glass windows in Chartres cathedral.

Attack on the Castle of Love, *lid from a jewelry casket, ca. 1330–1350 C.E. ivory with iron mounts.*

> *The two central panels show two knights jousting while their ladies watch from the balcony. All of the panels show themes that refer to love.*

Ivory carving

Ivory carving was common throughout the Middle Ages, but it reached a new height during the Gothic period. Ivory, taken from the tusks of elephants, was a highly prized material. It was used to make **devotional** sculptures and **secular** objects like the **casket** on this page. Ivory is a hard material, but it can be carved with sharp metal tools. It was carved into three-dimensional statues and carved into reliefs, or pictures that are carved to stand out from a stone, wood, or ivory background. Skilled artists could add many tiny details, such as fluttering flags or braided hair.

Using ivory
Small ivory panels with relief carvings were used on book covers, **reliquaries,** statues, and **crucifixes.** During the Gothic period, ivory was also used to make luxury items, including mirror cases, combs, and caskets for jewelry. The theme of the scenes on these objects was usually love.

ART FOR KINGS

Kings and other rulers had sculpture, **tapestries,** robes, crowns, and other kinds of art made for them. They preferred art that showed their power and their right to rule. There were many ways to do this. Many kings built huge palaces or castles and filled them with beautiful things like tapestries, books, and gold and silver objects. Another way of showing their strength as leaders was to pay for art that told stories of their military successes. Some of this art was displayed in the courts, while some was put into books for later rulers to see.

Kings also showed their power by buying things made out of expensive materials. Gold crowns studded with precious gems are one example. Kings, queens, and other leaders often wore robes made out of silk, fur, and other rich materials. Ordinary people weren't allowed to wear such things, and couldn't afford them anyway.

Blanche of Castile and King Louis IX of France, *page from a French Moralized Bible, ca. 1230 C.E.*

The wealth and power of the king of France and his mother are shown here by the rich colors of their clothing and by the gold background of the page.

Kings and the church

Another way for kings to show their strength was to buy art for churches. This showed the king's **devotion** to God. It also showed off his wealth.

Many kings argued for their right to rule by saying that God or Jesus approved of their leadership. For much of the Middle Ages, French kings were all crowned and buried in the same two churches. This was to show the people of France that God approved of the king's right to rule, and approved of the way the king had lived his life. Some kings also paid for art that showed God crowning them. This wasn't meant to be seen as a real event. Instead, it was a **symbol** of the king's right to rule.

Christ Crowning the Emperor Henry III and the Empress Agnes, *from the Uppsala Gospels, Echternach, Germany, completed in 1050 c.e.*

The powerful German emperor Henry III gave this book to the cathedral at Goslar. The painting shown here suggests that Jesus himself gave Henry the right to rule.

21

BEAUTIFUL BOOKS

In the Middle Ages, books were made by hand. Until the **Gothic** period, most books were made in **monasteries.** At first, only **monks** made books. During the Gothic period **universities** were built, and they began to replace monasteries as places for learning. **Secular** artists joined the monks in making books at this time, and eventually they took over the art of book making. At the very end of the Middle Ages, printed books were invented.

How books were made

Instead of paper, **medieval** books were made of sheets of **parchment** or **vellum.** Both of these were made with animal skins that had been scraped very thin. Scribes used ink to copy texts from older books. Then artists called **illuminators** painted small, brightly-colored illustrations, called **illuminations,** in these copies. The illumination on this page shows a scribe and an illuminator at work. More expensive books had another step, where gold was added to the illuminations. The whole process required careful planning, expensive materials, and a lot of time.

Scribe and illuminator in the monastery at Echternach, *Pericope Book, Germany, mid–eleventh century.*

The clothing of these men shows that the scribe is a secular artist and the illuminator is a monk.

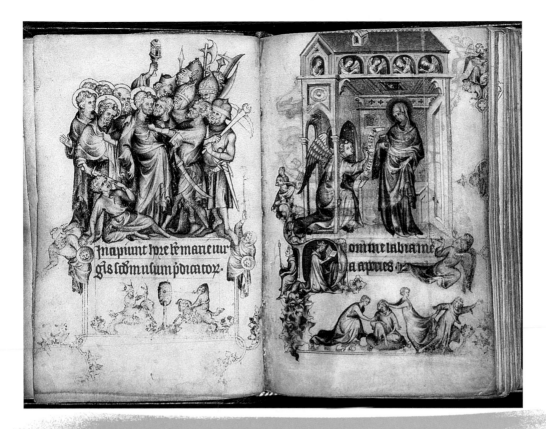

Illuminations from The Hours of Jeanne d'Evreux, *by Jean Pucelle, each page 3½ in. x 2½ in. (9 cm x 6 cm) ca. 1325–1328 C.E.*

The illuminator who illustrated this book was very famous. He added fanciful scenes around the edges of the pages. You can see the queen of France reading in the initial N.

Audiences for books

Illustrated books were luxury items during the Middle Ages. At first, books were only available to churches, monasteries, and royalty. These books contained stories from the Bible and other religious texts. Books that were made for churches were used in the **Mass.** Monks, nuns, and royalty used smaller books for personal prayer and **devotion.**

Later in the Middle Ages, noblemen and women were able to buy small books for personal use. The queen of France used the book shown on this page during her daily prayers. As more people learned to read, and the universities grew, there was greater demand for books. From about 1200 C.E. on, secular texts, including history, poetry, and stories, became common.

MEDIEVAL SCULPTURE

First the sculptor chose a block of stone or wood. An axe or **adze** was used to remove large pieces of material, leaving a rough outline of the shape. Next, the sculptor used a chisel to carve the surface until the sculpture was nearly done. Finally, special drills and tools were used to polish parts of the sculpture and add tiny details.

Romanesque sculpture

In **Romanesque** sculpture, monsters, animals, plants, and geometric designs are common features. People of all types appear regularly. Romanesque sculpture often showed storytelling scenes that were cleverly fitted inside frames. People and animals were shown in poses that hinted at their feelings.

The Romanesque period was also the first time that carved **portals** appeared in churches. These sculptures were very complex. They included stories from the Bible and often included zodiac symbols and symbols of the twelve months.

Prophet and lions, *south portal, Saint Pierre, Moissac, France, ca. 1115–1130 C.E.*

The sculptor carefully carved matching pairs of lions to fit inside the space of the door post. The sculptor also created a feeling of movement by making the lions lean forward.

Gothic sculpture

Portal sculpture continued to be favored in the **Gothic** period, but there was a greater sense of order. The people in the sculptures are less crowded in their settings. The figures in Gothic sculpture were more three-dimensional, and looked more like real people than the people in Romanesque sculpture.

During the Gothic period, wealthy people began to buy more sculptures. They preferred small sculptures, especially statues of religious figures like the Virgin Mary. They put these in their homes or gave them to churches.

Annunciation and Visitation, *center portal, west side, Reims Cathedral, France, ca. 1225–1245 C.E.*

The four figures look very calm and relaxed. You can tell that they are part of a Gothic sculpture because the figures look more lifelike.

PAINTED PICTURES

During the Middle Ages, painting wasn't as important as it is today. People preferred things like sculptures, books, and objects made out of gold and jewels over painting. One kind of painting that was important was the **illuminations** done to illustrate books. The other popular kind of painting was painting on walls. Many of these paintings were **frescoes.** Frescoes are pictures that are painted on walls while the plaster on the wall is still damp. The **pigments** in the paint bind to the plaster as it dries.

Unfortunately, most of the wall paintings from the Middle Ages have not survived. Only a few are left. We know about others from drawings and descriptions in books. Like most other art in the Middle Ages, wall paintings had religious subjects.

Painting on wood panels was another type of painting made in the Middle Ages. This kind of painting wasn't very common. But at the end of the Middle Ages, it began to be popular. This type of painting was often found in churches behind the altar. Painted panels for altars usually featured one holy person or saint in the center, with smaller story-telling scenes on the sides.

Artists used tempera, a mixture of egg yolk and pigment, for these panels. At the end of the Middle Ages, artists in the Netherlands and Germany began using oil mixed with pigment for their paints. This type of oil paint made the surface of the painting look very rich and shiny.

Noah's Ark, *fresco from the ceiling of the Church of Saint-Savin-sur-Gartempe, France, ca. 1100 C.E.*

This fresco shows a scene from the Biblical story of Noah. You can see the pairs of animals in the windows of the ark.

Make a Model Medieval Fresco

You will need:

cardboard
paper and pencil
string and scissors
poster paints
ruler and scotch tape

fine paint brush
cutting mat
plaster
mat knife

1. Sketch a design on scrap paper. Measure the design and make a cardboard mold the same size, with sides 2 in. (5 cm) deep. Score the sides, turn them up, and tape them together.

2. Mix the plaster in an old container according to the instructions on the package. Pour it into the mold to a depth of 1¼ in. (3 cm). Smooth the surface of the plaster. Cut a 6 in. (15 cm) piece of string and push the ends into the wet plaster leaving a loop to hang the finished fresco.

3. When the plaster is dry remove it from the mold. Trace your design onto the smooth surface. Pencil in the outline of your design. Apply a thin coat of wet plaster over the top. You should still be able to see the outline. Color in your design with the poster paints while the plaster topcoat is still damp.

THE END OF THE MIDDLE AGES

During the fourteenth century, the way people thought about their world and their lives began to change. These changes in the way people thought about things happened at the end of the Middle Ages, leading to a new period called the Renaissance. One of the most important changes was that people became more interested in the uniqueness of human beings.

A time of change

In the Middle Ages, a person was seen as a member of a group instead of an individual. In the Renaissance, it was believed that each person was unique. People also believed that human beings were the most special part of God's creation. Because of these changes, there was more interest in advancements people could make in science, medicine, and the arts.

Joachim among the Shepherds, *by Giotto, fresco, ca. 1305 C.E., Scrovegni (Arena) Chapel, Padua, Italy. 78³/₄ in. x 72⁷/₈ in. (200 cm x 185 cm).*

Giotto painted many different human emotions. Here he shows Joachim looking sad, while the shepherds look shy and uncomfortable. This picture is a good example of the way art looked at the end of the Middle Ages, since it shows both the new interest in lifelike painting and the old tradition of using a painting to teach people who is who in the church.

Transformations in art

The end of the Middle Ages was a time of **prosperity** in many countries. A new middle class developed, because of new trade and ways of doing business, and they had money to spend on art. This was different from most of the Middle Ages, when only churches, kings, and noblemen had enough money to buy art.

People who bought art, called patrons, became more interested in subjects that showed human feelings and activities. There was also a greater desire for art that looked more lifelike. This was related to the new interest in the lifelike and natural-looking art of ancient Greece and Rome.

The status of artists also changed. During the Middle Ages, artists were usually anonymous members of **guilds** or **monasteries.** In the Renaissance, the individual styles and personalities of artists became more and more important.

Saint Jerome in His Study, *by Antonello da Messina, oil on panel, Italy, ca.1450–1455 C.E., 18 in. x 14¹/₈ in. (46 cm x 36 cm).*

Antonello used new artistic techniques to make this painting look very lifelike. He used geometry to make it look like you could walk right into this room. He also included details of everyday life to show the saint's human qualities. If you look closely at the painting you can see that he included a lion, the symbol of St. Jerome.

TIMELINE

GLOSSARY

abbey religious center, usually with a church and monastery

abbot head of a monastery

adze cutting tool used for trimming pieces of stone or wood from a sculpture

apse semicircular east end of a church, where the altar is

artisan skilled person who makes crafts or art for a career, for example a book illustrator, woodcarver, or goldsmith

buttress sturdy stone support on the outside of a structure that holds up walls

casket small box that holds valuable objects

cathedral main church in a district

chapel small area in a church that is used for private prayer

crucifix sculpture or painting of Jesus on the cross

Crusades series of wars waged by Christian Europeans against Muslims in the Middle East

devotional related to prayer or religious feelings

enamel colored liquid that becomes smooth, shiny, and hard when heated

fresco painting made on a wall while the plaster is still damp

Gothic period in art that lasted from about 1150 C.E. to about 1400 C.E.

guild group of artisans and craftspeople

halo circle of light around the head of a saint or holy person

illumination small painting in a book

illuminator artisan or craftsman who specializes in painting illuminations

interlace pattern in jewelry or paintings that looks like ribbons woven together

lintel upper beam of a doorway

mandorla almond-shaped halo that goes around the whole body of an important holy person, usually Jesus

mason stoneworker who designed buildings and directed the workers who built them

Mass religious service in the Catholic church

medieval word used to describe something from the Middle Ages

migratory people with no settled home that travel from place to place

monastery group of buildings, including a church, where monks live

nave long, central aisle of a church that leads to the altar

Norman member of a group of people from what is now France

parchment thin paper-like sheets made from animal hides that have been scraped, treated, and trimmed

pigment colored material taken from animals, plants, earth, or rocks and used to make paint or dye

portal large doorway

prosperity wealth and success

relic remains of a holy person or saint

reliquary special container for relics, usually made of expensive materials

resurrection rebirth

Romanesque period in art and architecture that lasted from about 1050 to 1200 C.E.

Saxon member of a group of people from what is now Germany

secular something not part of or related to the church

symbolism when an object or a sign stands for something else

tapestry textile with woven pictures

tympanum space inside an arch over a doorway

university school that taught young men about the sciences, the church, and the history of thought

vellum paper-like material made from calfskin, like parchment, but softer and lighter

MORE BOOKS TO READ

Hinds, Kathryn. *Life in the Middle Ages: The Church*. New York: Marshall Cavendish, 2000.

Shuter, Jane. *The Middle Ages*. Chicago: Heinemann Library, 1998.

INDEX